The Castoff Canine

Written by Jeannette Elum Greulach

Illustrated by Amanda Morena

ISBN: 979-8-9937035-1-0

Dedication

This book is dedicated to my dogs, Rocky, Raven, and Vinny along with all the hard-working rescue animal volunteers and brave rescue animals. All the author/publisher net book proceeds will go to support these causes. This book is in memory of Rocky who passed away due to illness a year before publication.

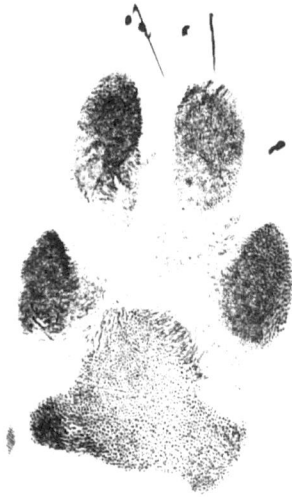

Rocky

Rocky was a dog living a lonely life outside.
He looked up at the stars each night and wished for a family. He saw dogs with families when he would take himself on walks. He wondered why his family hadn't found him yet. He had a family at one time, but he didn't know why they left him.

He wished and wished and the years passed.
As he grew, he wondered if he would ever find a family to love him.

One day a nice lady handed him a treat, and another, and another, until….He was in the back of her vehicle. Rocky didn't know where he was going. He was scared but thought just maybe he was on his way to find his family.

As the minutes turned into hours,
Rocky got nervous.

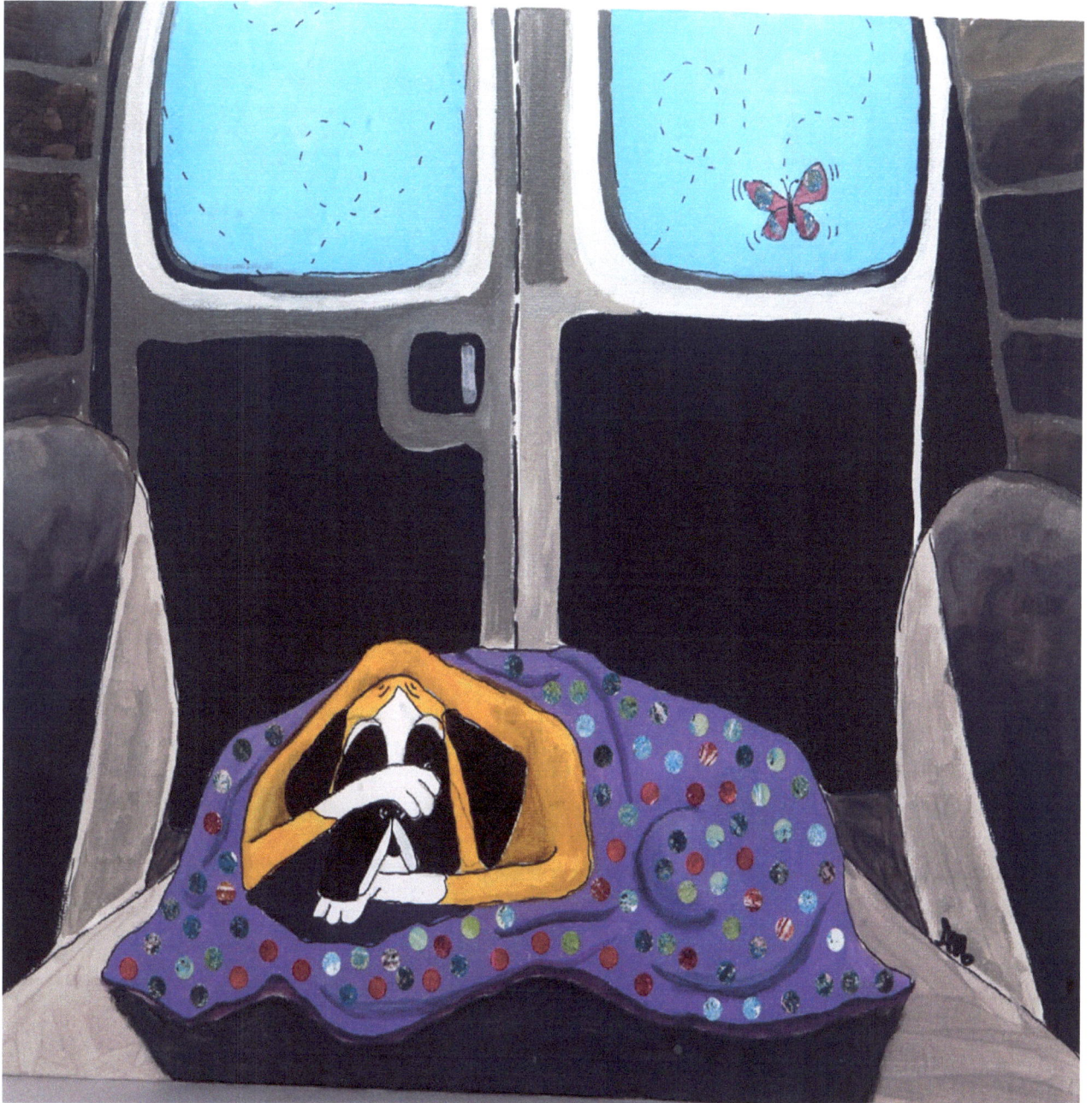

When the vehicle finally stopped, Rocky jumped out of the back. He looked around. There were many dogs, and it didn't appear that any of them had families.

Rocky thought that this must be the place for dogs without families. He put his head down as his dreams began to shatter. It seemed that he would never find a family. Why did no one want him?

The days turned into weeks.
The weeks turned into months.
One day Rocky was brought into the nice lady's office. It was nice here, he had food, water, and love but still no family. As he sat in the office a woman came in.

Rocky looked cautiously at the woman.
She slowly went up to him and tried to see if she could pet him. As
Rocky got more comfortable, the girl gave him a hug and kiss and
said,
"Welcome home sweet boy. I will love you forever."

Rocky slowly was introduced to the young woman's life. He met her parents who he called grandma & grandpa, her brother who was now his uncle, and her husband, who was now his dad.

It took some time to warm up to his sister, Raven, but with time she became his very best friend. Raven told him she was rescued too. She was found as a puppy on the side of the road and now has the best life.

Rocky learned that he also had fur cousins and so many family members he could hardly keep them all straight. He also had more friends than he ever thought possible. He learned many of his fur cousins and friends were rescued too. He started to feel like a normal dog, how he had always dreamed.

Rocky had to learn manners. Although he was 4 years old, he needed to learn to walk on a leash, potty outside, and most importantly, that he did not sleep outside. He had his very own bed next to his new sister in his parents' room.

He had a team of loving vets who helped keep him healthy and happy.

He had regular meals, water, trips to the doggy bakery, toys and most special of all, love.
Lots and lots of love.

After a year of training and work, Rocky became a therapy dog. His job was to go to work with his mom and brighten the days of others.

As the years passed, Rocky realized how loved he was every single day because he was saved first by his rescue and then by his forever family.
As he started to turn gray, he never missed a walk.
He had a job he loved, and family who loved him more than he ever thought was possible.

As he looked up at the same stars he had wished upon years before,
he said,
"Thank you for making me the luckiest rescue dog in the world, and
please find all the homeless dogs a loving home like mine."

Epilogue

Rocky and his mom volunteered to find homes for more dogs.
This book is based on a true story.
Rocky had a happy ending but there are so many dogs out there
waiting for YOU! Please consider fostering or adopting.

About the Author

Jeannette M. Elum Greulach grew up with her large loving family and two boxers, Duke and Champ, two rescue cats, Astro and Bella, a bunny named Snow White and other small pets in her hometown of Massillon, Ohio. When she was ready to have a dog of her own, she knew she wanted to rescue a boxer. From the second she saw Rocky on a Facebook post, she knew she needed him to be part of her family. Jeannette graduated from Miami University where she received her bachelor's degree in Health Science. She then went on to receive her MBA at Walsh University. Jeannette then moved to Boston, Massachusetts where she received a graduate certificate in Business Management from Harvard University while working at Tufts Medical Center. Jeannette returned to Ohio to work at The Ohio State University Wexner Medical Center. She adopted Rocky, a rescue boxer, as part of her family. Unfortunately, Rocky lost his battle with a heart condition and cancer in December 2024. He sat next to Jeannette as she wrote this book and she read it to him many times, including on his last day. Jeannette lives in Columbus, Ohio with her husband, Ryan, and their two dogs, Raven and Vinny.

About the Illustrator

Amanda Morena is a teaching artist who lives and works in her studio in downtown Canal Fulton, Ohio. She calls her Canal Fulton studio her illustration HQ. She lives with her two very artistic daughters and photographer George Bekich.

Amanda studied art and education at Kent State University. She taught preschool to her two daughters. "Miss Amanda" continues to teach preschoolers as well as adults art. Her public art career began by painting pet portraits for friends and family at The Hub in downtown Canton, Ohio. After that, her business grew. She has also volunteered and worked at the Canton Museum of Art in various roles from Japanese Tea Ceremony to Art Summer Camp! Amanda goes by the name A Lotus for studio work purposes.

Author Jeannette and Illustrator Amanda met through a pet portrait commission. Now they are a super children's book team!

You can follow A Lotus (Amanda Morena) on her website alotusdesigns.com.

Acknowledgments

I would first like to thank Shelly and the board at Canine Castaways Rescue in Fountaintown, Indiana for saving my sweet boys, Rocky and Vinny. Rocky grew with lots of training, love, and dedication. Rescue dogs do not come perfect, but they do come loving you with all they have. Rocky went through training and was accepted into Buckeye Paws, a program at The Ohio State University Wexner Medical Center. We are forever thankful to this program. I watched Rocky become more confident, and it made my day each time he was so proud to put on his uniform. He also volunteered visiting hospice patients at Capital City Hospice.

Thank you to his veterinarians, Dr. Huter, Dr. Nguyenba, Dr. Fine, Dr. Pogue, and their teams who helped him to be healthy and strong until his last breath. Also, kudos to these fine doctors for answering all my many questions to better my dog's health and wellness. Thank you to his trainers TranquilPax and TEAM K9 Academy along with our girl Raven's rescue, Cause For Canines in Columbus, Ohio. Rocky loved his sister Raven so much. Raven is in agility training at All Breeds Training.

Most importantly, I would like to thank my family, my husband, Ryan, my parents Eddie and Margaret, brother Paul, my in-laws Greg, Rosie, Janet, Jennifer, and Darin and all of my many cousins, aunts, and uncles; all of my wonderful friends for their love and support for me but also for my sweet dogs. A big thanks to Rocky's friends for giving him a chance, especially my brothers dog, Bruno-a rescued pit bull. Most of Rocky's friends are featured in this book. Every single picture has meaning and is a personal picture of someone or some place that has touched his life, with their approval of course! Thank you to my illustrator, Amanda. We met through my cousin who got me a group gift-a painting of Rocky. Since then, she has done paintings of our dogs, house, our first date spot, wedding, and countless gifts for family and friends. Thank you Mom and Aunt Arlene for editing and finally, a formal thank you to all of you for reading this book and to all of those who have rescued an animal or supported homeless pets.

My favorite saying is one hanging in my aunt and uncles' home, "Saving one dog will not change the world but surely for that one dog the world will change forever." I think of this each time I volunteer.

Special Note

Katherine Taylor Wilhelm and Champ perished in a fatal car accident.

Katherine is the one standing on the page where Rocky is picked up and her personal dog, Max is at the bottom left of Rocky's friend page. Max lived with his amazing foster family after the accident until he found his wonderful forever family. Katherine was also fostering a sweet dog named Zelena at the time, who was fostered and then adopted by an amazing family as well.

Champ was her other foster dog, and she was taking him to the vet for a newly diagnosed heart condition. A police officer at the scene helped the author track down Champ's body. The author arranged to have Champ cremated and picked up in Indiana. He's now resting easy with Rocky in the author's home. Their ashes share a shelf.

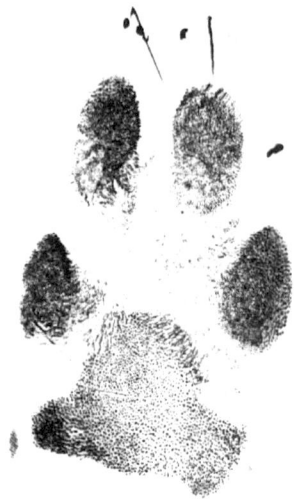

Rocky

www.ingramcontent.com/pod-product-compliance
Lightning Source LLC
Chambersburg PA
CBHW041428090426
42741CB00002B/86